# Sir Fluffy Versus Trump

Betty Smith
*Cat Lover*

# TABLE OF CONTENTS

# The Unlikely Challenger

In the bustling heart of the city,
nestled between towering buildings,

was a small animal shelter that was home to a host of furry residents. Among them was a particularly striking orange kitten named Sir Fluffy McWhiskerton. Sir Fluffy wasn't just any kitten; he was a feisty bundle of energy with fur as bright as a sunset and a spirit that refused to be caged.

On this particular day, Sir Fluffy was in the middle of his daily exercise routine. With a makeshift weight made of a small ball tied to a string, he was doing his 'kitty push-ups', a spectacle that amused both the shelter staff and his fellow furry inmates.

"Showing off those muscles again, eh, Fluffy?" a deep, amused voice boomed from the corner. It was General Barkington, an old but wise bulldog, known for his service in the K9 unit and his sagely advice. His face was grizzled, but his eyes sparkled with a youthful mischief.

Sir Fluffy paused and puffed out his chest, "I'm not just a pretty face, General. I'm building my strength. One day, I'll leap out of here and into a grand adventure!"

General Barkington chuckled, his jowls shaking. "Adventure, you say? Well, young Sir Fluffy, it just so happens that an opportunity has presented itself."

Sir Fluffy's ears perked up in interest. "An opportunity? Do tell, General!"

The old dog sauntered over, lowering his voice conspiratorially. "There's a charity boxing match coming up. It's all for a good cause, but here's the interesting part – the opponent is none other than Donald Trump."

Sir Fluffy's eyes widened, and he nearly lost his balance. "The Donald Trump? The one and only?"

"Exactly," General Barkington nodded, his tail wagging slowly. "Imagine, a little kitten like you in the ring with a big shot like him. It would be quite the sight, wouldn't it?"

Sir Fluffy's whiskers twitched with excitement. "But, why would they let me, a simple shelter kitten, box against someone so... so..."

"Infamous?" General Barkington offered with a grin.

"Exactly!" Sir Fluffy exclaimed. "It sounds absurd, yet thrilling!"

General Barkington's eyes twinkled with pride. "Well, they're looking for a challenger who's brave, charismatic, and has a fighting spirit. And you, Sir Fluffy, have all of that in spades."

Sir Fluffy puffed up, feeling a surge of determination. "You really think I could do it? Stand toe-to-toe with him in the ring?"

"Without a doubt," the old dog affirmed. "It's not about the size of the cat in the fight, but the size of the fight in the cat. And you, my little friend, have the heart of a lion."

Sir Fluffy's tail swished with newfound purpose. "Then I accept the challenge! I'll train, I'll fight, and I'll show the world what Sir Fluffy McWhiskerton is made of!"

General Barkington laughed heartily. "That's the spirit! Now, let's get you ready. We have a big match to prepare for!"

And with that, an unlikely champion began his journey, from a simple shelf in the animal shelter to the glaring lights of a boxing ring. Little did Sir Fluffy know, his adventure was just beginning.

# Challenge
# Accepted

The sun had barely risen, but the
animal shelter was already buzzing
with an unusual energy. News of Sir

Fluffy McWhiskerton's upcoming boxing match had spread like wildfire, not just within the walls of the shelter but far beyond.

In the early light, Sir Fluffy was hard at work, under the watchful eye of General Barkington. The old bulldog had taken it upon himself to be Sir Fluffy's coach, and he was determined to make a fighter out of the little kitten.

"You need to be quick, Fluffy! Dodge, weave, bob!" General Barkington instructed as Sir Fluffy darted around, playfully batting at a hanging feather duster.

"Like this, General?" Sir Fluffy panted, his orange fur a blur of motion.

"Exactly! Imagine that's Trump's hand reaching for you. You've got to be faster than his tweets!" General Barkington barked, unable to hide a smirk.

Sir Fluffy leaped high, swiping at the duster with a mock ferocity. "Take that, Mr. Trump!" he shouted, landing gracefully on his tiny paws.

"Now, don't get cocky," the old dog cautioned, "Remember, it's all in good fun, but we still have to show respect to our... unique opponent."

As they continued their training, a shelter volunteer snapped a photo of Sir Fluffy's boxing stance and posted it online. Within hours, it went viral. People couldn't get enough of the tiny, feisty kitten preparing to take on a former U.S. president.

Meanwhile, outside the shelter, a crowd of reporters and camera crews had gathered. The story of the kitten vs. the mogul had caught the imagination of the public, and everyone wanted a piece of it.

"Is it true that a kitten from this shelter is boxing Donald Trump for charity?" one reporter shouted, trying to get the attention of the shelter manager.

"Yes, it's true," the manager replied, bewildered by the attention. "Sir Fluffy McWhiskerton will be representing us. It's all in good fun and for a good cause."

Back inside, General Barkington looked out the window at the growing media frenzy. "Looks like you're a celebrity now, Fluffy."

Sir Fluffy, still panting from his training, peered out curiously. "Wow, so many humans! Do you think they all believe in me?"

"They're curious, that's for sure," General Barkington mused. "But whether they believe in you or not, we know you've got the heart and the spirit to make this a match to remember."

As the day turned into evening, the shelter was abuzz with excitement and speculation. The other animals watched Sir Fluffy with a mix of awe and amusement. He was, after all, one of their own, about to do something no one had ever dreamed of.

As Sir Fluffy curled up for the night, his dreams were filled with visions of the boxing ring, cheering crowds, and a bewildering yet exciting adventure ahead. This was more than just a match; it was his chance to shine, to prove that even the smallest among us could rise to extraordinary challenges.

# The Donald Prepares

The excitement surrounding the upcoming boxing match had reached fever pitch, and both competitors were deep in preparation, albeit in vastly different ways.

In a luxurious, opulent gym, Donald Trump was seen preparing for the match. Surrounded by a team of trainers, he seemed more focused on his appearance than on any actual boxing technique. He jabbed at the air, his movements more for show than effect, often pausing to admire himself in the mirror.

"Make sure you capture my good side," Trump instructed a photographer, flashing a confident grin. "This is going to be the easiest match ever. I mean, it's just a kitten, right? How hard can it be?"

His trainers exchanged uneasy glances but continued to offer praise and encouragement, more concerned with maintaining his ego than challenging his underestimation of Sir Fluffy.

Meanwhile, back at the shelter, Sir Fluffy was honing his own secret weapon. Throughout his training, both Sir Fluffy and General Barkington had noticed something peculiar about the kitten's fur. It seemed to generate a considerable amount of static electricity, enough to give a surprising little zap to anyone who touched it.

"Your fur might just be your ace in the hole, Fluffy," General Barkington remarked as he watched the kitten scurry across a carpet, building up static.

Sir Fluffy, charged with energy, both literal and figurative, zapped a nearby ball of yarn, sending it rolling across the floor. "Zap! Take that, Mr. Trump!" he exclaimed with glee.

General Barkington chuckled. "Just remember, we're not looking to hurt anyone. It's all in good fun. But a little shock might just give you the edge you need to distract him."

As the day of the match drew closer, the world watched with bated breath. Some saw the event as a mere publicity stunt, a bit of light-hearted entertainment. Others were genuinely curious about how this unusual matchup would unfold.

In their respective corners, both Trump and Sir Fluffy continued their preparation. Trump, with his overconfidence and flair for the dramatic, and Sir Fluffy, with his quick paws, sharp instincts, and surprisingly zappy fur.

The stage was set for a confrontation that was anything but conventional. It was shaping up to be a match that would be talked about for years to come, a true clash of the unexpected.

# Pre-Match Jitters

The night before the big match, the atmosphere at the animal shelter was tense and electric. Sir Fluffy, nestled in his cozy bed in the locker room, tried to appear calm, but his twitching whiskers betrayed his nervousness.

General Barkington, ever the stoic mentor, sat beside him, offering a comforting presence. "Remember, Fluffy, it's not just about winning. It's about showing the world what you're made of," he said, his voice steady and reassuring.

Just then, a shelter volunteer turned on the TV for the evening news. The lead story was, unsurprisingly, the upcoming match. The reporter announced that Donald Trump had sent a message to his opponent.

On the screen, Trump appeared, his expression smug. "I hope that little kitten is ready for tomorrow. I'm not just any opponent – I'm Donald Trump, and I don't lose. See you in the ring, Fluffy."

Sir Fluffy's ears flattened against his head. The confidence he had felt during training began to waver. He looked up at General Barkington, his green eyes filled with doubt. "General, what if I can't do this? What if he's right?"

General Barkington let out a soft, reassuring growl. "Don't let his words get to you, Fluffy. He's trying to intimidate you, to make you doubt yourself. But remember, courage isn't the absence of fear. It's facing your fears and standing tall despite them."

Sir Fluffy took a deep breath, trying to internalize the old dog's words. "I'm just a kitten from a shelter. Can I really stand up to someone like him?"

"You're much more than just a kitten, Fluffy. You're a symbol of hope and courage to all of us here," General Barkington said, his gaze unwavering. "You've already won by stepping into that ring. No matter what happens, you've shown us that even the smallest among us can rise to the biggest challenges."

The words settled over Sir Fluffy like a warm blanket, easing his fears. He looked at his reflection in a small mirror, his fur fluffed up, his stance strong. He might have been small, but his heart was as big as any champion's.

As the night wore on, the shelter settled into a quiet hush. Sir Fluffy, feeling a renewed sense of purpose, curled up beside General Barkington, the old dog's steady breathing a comforting rhythm in the dark.

Tomorrow was a big day, a day that might just change his life forever. But whatever happened, Sir Fluffy knew he wouldn't be facing it alone. He had found courage, friendship, and a

sense of belonging, and that was
worth more than any title or trophy.

# The Big Event

The day of the match had arrived, and the air was thick with anticipation. The arena was packed with an eclectic mix of spectators, all eager to witness the most bizarre boxing match in history.

First to make his entrance was Donald Trump, accompanied by a dramatic overture. He strutted down the aisle with exaggerated confidence, his hair impeccably styled in its signature whoosh, almost a character in its own right. The crowd responded with a mixture of cheers and laughter, the spectacle of it all too surreal to fully grasp.

Then came Sir Fluffy's turn. The arena lights dimmed, and a single spotlight focused on the entrance. With a triumphant fanfare, Sir Fluffy emerged, carried on a small, decorated platform by volunteers from the shelter. His fur was groomed to perfection, mirroring the flamboyant style of his opponent's hair, creating an amusing visual parallel that didn't go unnoticed by the audience.

As Sir Fluffy was placed in the ring, the two competitors faced each other for the first time. Trump, towering over the tiny kitten, couldn't help but smirk. "Ready to lose, Fluffy?" he taunted.

Sir Fluffy, undeterred, puffed up his fur, making himself look as big as possible. "I may be small, but I've got a big heart. And some pretty shocking fur!" he retorted, causing a ripple of laughter through the crowd.

The bell rang, signaling the start of the first round. Trump, still underestimating Sir Fluffy, reached out to give what he thought would be a gentle tap. But Sir Fluffy was quicker than he appeared. With a nimble leap, he dodged Trump's hand, landing a few feet away with a triumphant flick of his tail.

Trump, taken aback, tried again, only to be met with the same result. Sir Fluffy was a blur of orange, darting this way and that, his movements almost a dance. The crowd was in stitches, the absurdity of the situation enhanced by the comical contrast between the two.

"Not so easy to catch, am I?" Sir Fluffy teased, his confidence growing with each successful dodge.

Trump, now slightly flustered, adjusted his hair, which had started to lose its perfect shape. "You're quicker than I thought, kitten. But this is just the warm-up!"

As the round progressed, it became clear that this was no ordinary match. It was a spectacle, a clash of styles and personalities, underlined by the unlikely similarity of their flamboyant hairdos. Sir Fluffy, with his agility and surprising quickness, and Trump, with his larger-than-life persona, provided a show that was as entertaining as it was unprecedented.

As the bell rang to signal the end of the first round, both competitors retreated to their corners, their hair – one natural, one not so much – a testament to the wild and whimsical nature of the event. The crowd was buzzing, already wondering what the next round would bring in this most unusual of boxing matches.

# The Unexpected Turn

As the second round commenced, the energy in the arena was electric – quite literally, as it would soon become apparent. Sir Fluffy, energized by his performance in the first round, was ready to up the ante.

"Ready for round two, Mr. Trump?" Sir Fluffy called out, his fur standing on end, not just from excitement but also from the static electricity he had been building up.

Trump, determined to regain his composure, stepped forward. "This time, you won't be so lucky, Fluffy."

But as he reached out towards Sir Fluffy, something unexpected happened. Trump's hair, already a bit disheveled from the first round, began to react to the static in the air. It started to lift, slowly at first, then more noticeably, standing almost on end, much to the amazement and amusement of the spectators.

"What in the...?" Trump stammered, trying to pat his hair down, but it only seemed to worsen.

Sir Fluffy, seeing the opportunity, darted close to Trump, the static from his fur exacerbating the situation. With each pass, Trump's hair became more and more unruly, defying gravity in a bizarre and hilarious spectacle.

The crowd roared with laughter as Trump became increasingly flustered, his attempts to control his hair failing comically. "This isn't part of the plan!" he exclaimed, his image of unflappable confidence crumbling.

Sir Fluffy, meanwhile, was having the time of his life. "Looks like your hair is a bigger fan of me than you are!" he quipped, bouncing around the ring, his own fur poofed out in all its static glory.

The match had turned into a slapstick comedy, with Trump's hair becoming the unintentional star of the show. Each attempt by Trump to land a gentle tap on Sir Fluffy only resulted in more hair-raising antics, literally.

As the round drew to a close, Trump's hair had taken on a life of its own, standing out in all directions, much to the delight of the crowd. Sir Fluffy, on the other paw, looked as fluffy and electrifying as ever, his fur a static masterpiece.

The bell rang, and both competitors, one ruffled, one fluffed, retreated to their corners. The arena was alive with laughter and cheers, the spectacle far exceeding anyone's expectations. This wasn't just a boxing match anymore; it had become a legendary comedy show, all thanks to a feisty orange kitten and some unruly hair.

# The **Winning** Way

The third round was about to begin, and the atmosphere in the arena was one of sheer anticipation. In Sir Fluffy's corner, however, there was a touch of concern. General Barkington was looking a bit under the weather, his usually bright eyes dimmed with fatigue.

"Are you okay, General?" Sir Fluffy asked, his concern evident.

"I'll be fine, Fluffy. Just a bit of a cold," the old dog replied, trying to sound more robust than he felt. "But you, young warrior, you need to focus on the match. I believe in you."

Sir Fluffy nodded, a determined glint in his eyes. He turned to face Trump, who was looking increasingly uneasy. As Sir Fluffy approached, Trump began to cough and wheeze, his face turning a shade redder than usual.

"Seems like Mr. Trump is allergic to cats," a volunteer whispered, a realization that quickly spread through the crowd.

Trump, trying to maintain his composure, waved off his trainers who looked concerned. "I'm fine, let's just get this over with," he grumbled.

As the round started, Sir Fluffy used his quickness to his advantage, darting around Trump, who was now struggling with both his hair and his apparent allergy. With each pass, Trump's coughing and sneezing grew worse, his attempts to swat at Sir Fluffy becoming more desperate and less coordinated.

Sir Fluffy, sensing his opportunity, made his move. He leaped high into the air, his fur fully charged with static, and as he passed by Trump, his fur caused a final, catastrophic malfunction to Trump's hair. It stood up on end, stiff and static, like a bizarre crown.

The sight was too much for the audience, who erupted into uncontrollable laughter. Trump, now completely overwhelmed by his allergies and his rebellious hair, stumbled back, waving a white handkerchief in defeat.

"I surrender! I can't... ah-choo!... do this anymore!" he managed to say between sneezes.

Sir Fluffy landed gracefully, his mission accomplished. The crowd cheered wildly, chanting his name. He had done it; he had won against all odds.

In his corner, General Barkington mustered the strength to stand, pride shining in his eyes. "You did it, Fluffy. You showed them the heart of a champion."

Sir Fluffy, his fur still crackling with static, looked over at General Barkington. "I did it for us, General. For all of us in the shelter."

As the announcer declared Sir Fluffy the victor, the little orange kitten basked in the adoration of the crowd. He had not only won the match but had also won the hearts of everyone who witnessed his incredible journey.

Trump, still sneezing and trying to tame his hair, showed a rare moment of humility. "Well, I never thought I'd be bested by a kitten," he said, managing a begrudging smile.

The event ended not just as a victory for Sir Fluffy, but as a heartwarming reminder of the unexpected wonders that can come from the smallest and most unlikely of heroes.

# The Aftermath

The boxing ring was abuzz with
excitement and disbelief. Sir Fluffy,
the little orange kitten from the
shelter, had just accomplished the

impossible. He was being hoisted up by the shelter volunteers, a tiny champion in a sea of adoration.

General Barkington, feeling much better after witnessing the victory, stood by Sir Fluffy's side, his chest swelling with pride. "You did it, Sir Fluffy. You've shown the world what we're made of," he barked, his tail wagging vigorously.

Amidst the celebration, Donald Trump, looking more disheveled than ever, his hair in complete disarray and his face glistening with sweat, approached Sir Fluffy. He seemed to have shed his usual persona and was almost childlike in his demeanor.

"You know, Sir Fluffy, I think I'm gonna give up boxing," Trump said in a surprisingly light-hearted tone. "It's too sweaty, and my hair gets all messy. I think I should stick to being a president. It's easier than boxing with kittens!"

The crowd chuckled at Trump's words, a rare moment of self-deprecating humor from the former president. Sir Fluffy, still being celebrated, looked at Trump with a newfound respect.

"Mr. Trump, you were a good sport," Sir Fluffy meowed. "Thank you for helping us raise awareness for the shelter."

Trump, for a moment, looked genuinely touched. "Well, I never knew a kitten could be so tough. You've done a good thing here, Fluffy. Maybe I'll visit the shelter sometime, but next time, no boxing!"

The event ended on a high note, with laughter and good spirits all around. Sir Fluffy was the hero of the hour, his victory a symbol of hope and perseverance. The shelter received an outpouring of support and donations, and the story of the kitten who beat Donald Trump in a boxing match became an instant legend.

As the crowd dispersed, Sir Fluffy sat beside General Barkington, looking out at the arena now emptying rapidly. "We did something great today, General," Sir Fluffy purred contentedly.

"Yes, we did, Sir Fluffy. Yes, we did," General Barkington replied, a twinkle in his eye. "You've made us all proud."

And as they walked back to the shelter, the setting sun cast long shadows behind them, but the future seemed brighter than ever for Sir Fluffy McWhiskerton and all his friends at the shelter.

# A New Beginning

In the days following the match, Sir Fluffy McWhiskerton became a sensation far beyond the walls of the animal shelter. The story of the little kitten who bravely boxed against a former president had captured hearts everywhere.

It wasn't long before a family, who had watched the match with bated breath, came to the shelter. They had fallen in love with Sir Fluffy's courage and charm and wanted to give him a forever home. Sir Fluffy, with his usual mix of excitement and grace, embraced his new family, ready to start a new chapter in his life.

Meanwhile, the shelter was thriving. Donations poured in from all corners, and the publicity from the match brought awareness to the many other animals in need of homes.

General Barkington, now a celebrity in his own right, became the unofficial mascot of the shelter, his wisdom and warmth touching all who visited.

In his new home, Sir Fluffy found not just comfort and love but also a sense of belonging. He had a special place in the hearts of his family, and his story of bravery and resilience continued to inspire.

One evening, as Sir Fluffy curled up on the couch with his new family, they decided to watch a rerun of the match on ESPN. General Barkington, invited over for the special viewing, sat beside Sir Fluffy, both of them watching the screen with amusement.

As they watched the match, reliving each hilarious moment, their laughter filled the room. The sight of Trump's hair standing on end, his surprised expressions, and Sir Fluffy's agile maneuvers brought back a flood of happy memories.

"You were quite the opponent, Mr. Trump," Sir Fluffy chuckled, his eyes twinkling with mirth.

"And you, Sir Fluffy, were an unexpected champion," General Barkington added, his tail wagging.

Meanwhile, in a luxurious residence, Donald Trump himself was watching the same rerun. Seated rather unceremoniously on the toilet, he chuckled at the sight of himself on the screen, his hair in complete disarray.

"Well, I'll be," he mused aloud. "That kitten really did a number on me. Maybe I should stick to golf."

As the program ended, Sir Fluffy looked around at his loving family, his heart full of joy. He had gone from a shelter kitten to a celebrated hero, and now, he was simply a beloved pet, cherished and adored.

The story of Sir Fluffy McWhiskerton had become a tale of hope, laughter, and the unexpected twists of life. As he settled into a contented purr, surrounded by warmth and affection, he knew he had found his true home, his journey a remarkable testament to the saying that even the smallest can achieve the greatest.

## THE END

# Please, I Need Your Help

If you enjoyed **Sir Fluffy Versus Donald Trump** then please leave a review…

It will take you less than 60 seconds!

I read them all.

It really does matter!

Thank you so much.

- Betty Smith (Cat Lover)

Printed in Great Britain
by Amazon

35453837R00036